Cleaning TRACKER

THIS PLANNER BELONGS TO

. . . .

CLEANING TRACK

MONDAY
LIVING ROOM DAY

- [ ] . . . .
- [ ] . . . .
- [ ] . . . .
- [ ] . . . .
- [ ] . . . .
- [ ] . . . .

TUESDAY
KITCHEN DAY

- [ ] . . . .
- [ ] . . . .
- [ ] . . . .
- [ ] . . . .
- [ ] . . . .
- [ ] . . . .

WEDNESDAY
BEDROOM DAY

- [ ] . . . .
- [ ] . . . .
- [ ] . . . .
- [ ] . . . .
- [ ] . . . .
- [ ] . . . .

THUREDAY
LAUNDRY DAY

- [ ] . . . .
- [ ] . . . .
- [ ] . . . .
- [ ] . . . .
- [ ] . . . .
- [ ] . . . .

FRIDAY
BATHROOM DAY

- [ ] . . . .
- [ ] . . . .
- [ ] . . . .
- [ ] . . . .
- [ ] . . . .
- [ ] . . . .

SATURDAY
OUTSIDE

- [ ] . . . .
- [ ] . . . .
- [ ] . . . .
- [ ] . . . .
- [ ] . . . .
- [ ] . . . .

TO DO LIST EVERY DAY

- □ . . . .
- □ . . . .
- □ . . . .
- □ . . . .
- □ . . . .
- □ . . . .
- □ . . . .
- □ . . . .
- □ . . . .
- □ . . . .
- □ . . . .
- □ . . . .
- □ . . . .
- □ . . . .
- □ . . . .
- □ . . . .

NOTES

CLEANING TRACK

MONDAY
LIVING ROOM DAY

- ☐ . . . .
- ☐ . . . .
- ☐ . . . .
- ☐ . . . .
- ☐ . . . .
- ☐ . . . .

TUESDAY
KITCHEN DAY

- ☐ . . . .
- ☐ . . . .
- ☐ . . . .
- ☐ . . . .
- ☐ . . . .
- ☐ . . . .

WEDNESDAY
BEDROOM DAY

- ☐ . . . .
- ☐ . . . .
- ☐ . . . .
- ☐ . . . .
- ☐ . . . .
- ☐ . . . .

THUREDAY
LAUNDRY DAY

- ☐ . . . .
- ☐ . . . .
- ☐ . . . .
- ☐ . . . .
- ☐ . . . .

FRIDAY
BATHROOM DAY

- ☐ . . . .
- ☐ . . . .
- ☐ . . . .
- ☐ . . . .
- ☐ . . . .

SATURDAY
OUTSIDE

- ☐ . . . .
- ☐ . . . .
- ☐ . . . .
- ☐ . . . .
- ☐ . . . .

TO DO LIST EVERY DAY

- [ ] . . . .
- [ ] . . . .
- [ ] . . . .
- [ ] . . . .
- [ ] . . . .
- [ ] . . . .
- [ ] . . . .
- [ ] . . . .
- [ ] . . . .
- [ ] . . . .
- [ ] . . . .
- [ ] . . . .
- [ ] . . . .
- [ ] . . . .
- [ ] . . . .

NOTES

CLEANING TRACK

MONDAY
LIVING ROOM DAY

- [ ] . . . .
- [ ] . . . .
- [ ] . . . .
- [ ] . . . .
- [ ] . . . .
- [ ] . . . .

TUESDAY
KITCHEN DAY

- [ ] . . . .
- [ ] . . . .
- [ ] . . . .
- [ ] . . . .
- [ ] . . . .
- [ ] . . . .

WEDNESDAY
BEDROOM DAY

- [ ] . . . .
- [ ] . . . .
- [ ] . . . .
- [ ] . . . .
- [ ] . . . .
- [ ] . . . .

THUREDAY
LAUNDRY DAY

- [ ] . . . .
- [ ] . . . .
- [ ] . . . .
- [ ] . . . .
- [ ] . . . .
- [ ] . . . .

FRIDAY
BATHROOM DAY

- [ ] . . . .
- [ ] . . . .
- [ ] . . . .
- [ ] . . . .
- [ ] . . . .

SATURDAY
OUTSIDE

- [ ] . . . .
- [ ] . . . .
- [ ] . . . .
- [ ] . . . .
- [ ] . . . .

TO DO LIST EVERY DAY

- [ ] . . . .
- [ ] . . . .
- [ ] . . . .
- [ ] . . . .
- [ ] . . . .
- [ ] . . . .
- [ ] . . . .
- [ ] . . . .
- [ ] . . . .
- [ ] . . . .
- [ ] . . . .
- [ ] . . . .
- [ ] . . . .
- [ ] . . . .
- [ ] . . . .

NOTES

 # CLEANING TRACK

MONDAY
LIVING ROOM DAY

- . . . .
- . . . .
- . . . .
- . . . .
- . . . .
- . . . .

TUESDAY
KITCHEN DAY

- . . . .
- . . . .
- . . . .
- . . . .
- . . . .
- . . . .

WEDNESDAY
BEDROOM DAY

- . . . .
- . . . .
- . . . .
- . . . .
- . . . .
- . . . .

THUREDAY
LAUNDRY DAY

- . . . .
- . . . .
- . . . .
- . . . .
- . . . .
- . . . .

FRIDAY
BATHROOM DAY

- . . . .
- . . . .
- . . . .
- . . . .
- . . . .
- . . . .

SATURDAY
OUTSIDE

- . . . .
- . . . .
- . . . .
- . . . .
- . . . .
- . . . .

TO DO LIST EVERY DAY

- ☐ . . . .
- ☐ . . . .
- ☐ . . . .
- ☐ . . . .
- ☐ . . . .
- ☐ . . . .
- ☐ . . . .
- ☐ . . . .
- ☐ . . . .
- ☐ . . . .
- ☐ . . . .
- ☐ . . . .
- ☐ . . . .
- ☐ . . . .
- ☐ . . . .
- ☐ . . . .

NOTES

CLEANING TRACK

MONDAY
LIVING ROOM DAY

TUESDAY
KITCHEN DAY

WEDNESDAY
BEDROOM DAY

THUREDAY
LAUNDRY DAY

FRIDAY
BATHROOM DAY

SATURDAY
OUTSIDE

TO DO LIST EVERY DAY

- ·
- ·
- ·
- ·
- ·
- ·
- ·
- ·
- ·
- ·
- ·
- ·
- ·
- ·

NOTES

CLEANING TRACK

MONDAY
LIVING ROOM DAY

- ·
- ·
- ·
- ·
- ·
- ·

TUESDAY
KITCHEN DAY

- ·
- ·
- ·
- ·
- ·
- ·

WEDNESDAY
BEDROOM DAY

- ·
- ·
- ·
- ·
- ·
- ·

THUREDAY
LAUNDRY DAY

- ·
- ·
- ·
- ·
- ·
- ·

FRIDAY
BATHROOM DAY

- ·
- ·
- ·
- ·
- ·
- ·

SATURDAY
OUTSIDE

- ·
- ·
- ·
- ·
- ·
- ·

TO DO LIST EVERY DAY

- . . . .
- . . . .
- . . . .
- . . . .
- . . . .
- . . . .
- . . . .
- . . . .
- . . . .
- . . . .
- . . . .
- . . . .
- . . . .
- . . . .
- . . . .
- . . . .

NOTES

CLEANING TRACK

MONDAY
LIVING ROOM DAY

- ....
- ....
- ....
- ....
- ....
- ....

TUESDAY
KITCHEN DAY

- ....
- ....
- ....
- ....
- ....
- ....

WEDNESDAY
BEDROOM DAY

- ....
- ....
- ....
- ....
- ....
- ....

THUREDAY
LAUNDRY DAY

- ....
- ....
- ....
- ....
- ....
- ....

FRIDAY
BATHROOM DAY

- ....
- ....
- ....
- ....
- ....
- ....

SATURDAY
OUTSIDE

- ....
- ....
- ....
- ....
- ....
- ....

TO DO LIST EVERY DAY

- [ ] . . . .
- [ ] . . . .
- [ ] . . . .
- [ ] . . . .
- [ ] . . . .
- [ ] . . . .
- [ ] . . . .
- [ ] . . . .
- [ ] . . . .
- [ ] . . . .
- [ ] . . . .
- [ ] . . . .
- [ ] . . . .
- [ ] . . . .
- [ ] . . . .

NOTES

 # CLEANING TRACK

MONDAY
LIVING ROOM DAY

- [ ] ....
- [ ] ....
- [ ] ....
- [ ] ....
- [ ] ....
- [ ] ....

TUESDAY
KITCHEN DAY

- [ ] ....
- [ ] ....
- [ ] ....
- [ ] ....
- [ ] ....
- [ ] ....

WEDNESDAY
BEDROOM DAY

- [ ] ....
- [ ] ....
- [ ] ....
- [ ] ....
- [ ] ....

THUREDAY
LAUNDRY DAY

- [ ] ....
- [ ] ....
- [ ] ....
- [ ] ....
- [ ] ....

FRIDAY
BATHROOM DAY

- [ ] ....
- [ ] ....
- [ ] ....
- [ ] ....
- [ ] ....

SATURDAY
OUTSIDE

- [ ] ....
- [ ] ....
- [ ] ....
- [ ] ....
- [ ] ....

TO DO LIST EVERY DAY

- ·
- ·
- ·
- ·
- ·
- ·
- ·
- ·
- ·
- ·
- ·
- ·
- ·
- ·
- ·

NOTES

 # CLEANING TRACK

MONDAY
LIVING ROOM DAY

- ☐ . . . .
- ☐ . . . .
- ☐ . . . .
- ☐ . . . .
- ☐ . . . .
- ☐ . . . .

TUESDAY
KITCHEN DAY

- ☐ . . . .
- ☐ . . . .
- ☐ . . . .
- ☐ . . . .
- ☐ . . . .
- ☐ . . . .

WEDNESDAY
BEDROOM DAY

- ☐ . . . .
- ☐ . . . .
- ☐ . . . .
- ☐ . . . .
- ☐ . . . .
- ☐ . . . .

THUREDAY
LAUNDRY DAY

- ☐ . . . .
- ☐ . . . .
- ☐ . . . .
- ☐ . . . .
- ☐ . . . .
- ☐ . . . .

FRIDAY
BATHROOM DAY

- ☐ . . . .
- ☐ . . . .
- ☐ . . . .
- ☐ . . . .
- ☐ . . . .

SATURDAY
OUTSIDE

- ☐ . . . .
- ☐ . . . .
- ☐ . . . .
- ☐ . . . .
- ☐ . . . .

TO DO LIST EVERY DAY

- ·
- ·
- ·
- ·
- ·
- ·
- ·
- ·
- ·
- ·
- ·
- ·
- ·
- ·
- ·

NOTES

 # CLEANING TRACK

MONDAY
LIVING ROOM DAY

TUESDAY
KITCHEN DAY

WEDNESDAY
BEDROOM DAY

THUREDAY
LAUNDRY DAY

FRIDAY
BATHROOM DAY

SATURDAY
OUTSIDE

TO DO LIST EVERY DAY

- [ ] . . . .
- [ ] . . . .
- [ ] . . . .
- [ ] . . . .
- [ ] . . . .
- [ ] . . . .
- [ ] . . . .
- [ ] . . . .
- [ ] . . . .
- [ ] . . . .
- [ ] . . . .
- [ ] . . . .
- [ ] . . . .
- [ ] . . . .
- [ ] . . . .

NOTES

 # CLEANING TRACK

MONDAY
LIVING ROOM DAY

- ·
- ·
- ·
- ·
- ·
- ·

TUESDAY
KITCHEN DAY

- ·
- ·
- ·
- ·
- ·
- ·

WEDNESDAY
BEDROOM DAY

- ·
- ·
- ·
- ·
- ·
- ·

THUREDAY
LAUNDRY DAY

- ·
- ·
- ·
- ·
- ·
- ·

FRIDAY
BATHROOM DAY

- ·
- ·
- ·
- ·
- ·
- ·

SATURDAY
OUTSIDE

- ·
- ·
- ·
- ·
- ·
- ·

TO DO LIST EVERY DAY

- . . . .
- . . . .
- . . . .
- . . . .
- . . . .
- . . . .
- . . . .
- . . . .
- . . . .
- . . . .
- . . . .
- . . . .
- . . . .
- . . . .
- . . . .

NOTES

 # CLEANING TRACK

MONDAY
LIVING ROOM DAY

- ·
- ·
- ·
- ·
- ·
- ·

TUESDAY
KITCHEN DAY

- ·
- ·
- ·
- ·
- ·
- ·

WEDNESDAY
BEDROOM DAY

- ·
- ·
- ·
- ·
- ·
- ·

THUREDAY
LAUNDRY DAY

- ·
- ·
- ·
- ·
- ·
- ·

FRIDAY
BATHROOM DAY

- ·
- ·
- ·
- ·
- ·
- ·

SATURDAY
OUTSIDE

- ·
- ·
- ·
- ·
- ·
- ·

TO DO LIST EVERY DAY

- ☐ . . . .
- ☐ . . . .
- ☐ . . . .
- ☐ . . . .
- ☐ . . . .
- ☐ . . . .
- ☐ . . . .
- ☐ . . . .
- ☐ . . . .
- ☐ . . . .
- ☐ . . . .
- ☐ . . . .
- ☐ . . . .
- ☐ . . . .
- ☐ . . . .
- ☐ . . . .

NOTES

 # CLEANING TRACK

MONDAY
LIVING ROOM DAY

- ....
- ....
- ....
- ....
- ....
- ....

TUESDAY
KITCHEN DAY

- ....
- ....
- ....
- ....
- ....
- ....

WEDNESDAY
BEDROOM DAY

- ....
- ....
- ....
- ....
- ....
- ....

THUREDAY
LAUNDRY DAY

- ....
- ....
- ....
- ....
- ....
- ....

FRIDAY
BATHROOM DAY

- ....
- ....
- ....
- ....
- ....

SATURDAY
OUTSIDE

- ....
- ....
- ....
- ....
- ....

TO DO LIST EVERY DAY

- ☐ . . . .
- ☐ . . . .
- ☐ . . . .
- ☐ . . . .
- ☐ . . . .
- ☐ . . . .
- ☐ . . . .
- ☐ . . . .
- ☐ . . . .
- ☐ . . . .
- ☐ . . . .
- ☐ . . . .
- ☐ . . . .
- ☐ . . . .

NOTES

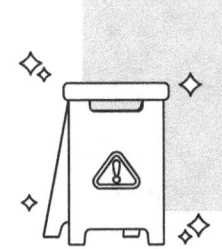
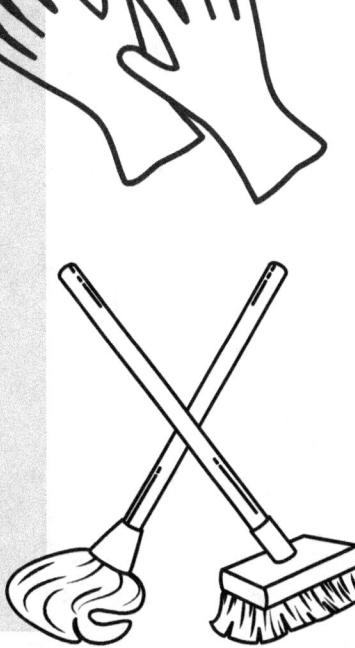

CLEANING TRACK

MONDAY
LIVING ROOM DAY

TUESDAY
KITCHEN DAY

WEDNESDAY
BEDROOM DAY

THUREDAY
LAUNDRY DAY

FRIDAY
BATHROOM DAY

SATURDAY
OUTSIDE

TO DO LIST EVERY DAY

- ·
- ·
- ·
- ·
- ·
- ·
- ·
- ·
- ·
- ·
- ·
- ·
- ·
- ·
- ·

NOTES

# CLEANING TRACK

MONDAY
LIVING ROOM DAY

- ⬛ . . . .
- ⬛ . . . .
- ⬛ . . . .
- ⬛ . . . .
- ⬛ . . . .
- ⬛ . . . .

TUESDAY
KITCHEN DAY

- ⬛ . . . .
- ⬛ . . . .
- ⬛ . . . .
- ⬛ . . . .
- ⬛ . . . .
- ⬛ . . . .

WEDNESDAY
BEDROOM DAY

- ⬛ . . . .
- ⬛ . . . .
- ⬛ . . . .
- ⬛ . . . .
- ⬛ . . . .
- ⬛ . . . .

THUREDAY
LAUNDRY DAY

- ⬛ . . . .
- ⬛ . . . .
- ⬛ . . . .
- ⬛ . . . .
- ⬛ . . . .
- ⬛ . . . .

FRIDAY
BATHROOM DAY

- ⬛ . . . .
- ⬛ . . . .
- ⬛ . . . .
- ⬛ . . . .
- ⬛ . . . .
- ⬛ . . . .

SATURDAY
OUTSIDE

- ⬛ . . . .
- ⬛ . . . .
- ⬛ . . . .
- ⬛ . . . .
- ⬛ . . . .
- ⬛ . . . .

TO DO LIST EVERY DAY

- □ . . . .
- □ . . . .
- □ . . . .
- □ . . . .
- □ . . . .
- □ . . . .
- □ . . . .
- □ . . . .
- □ . . . .
- □ . . . .
- □ . . . .
- □ . . . .
- □ . . . .
- □ . . . .
- □ . . . .

NOTES

 # CLEANING TRACK

MONDAY
LIVING ROOM DAY

- ☐ . . . .
- ☐ . . . .
- ☐ . . . .
- ☐ . . . .
- ☐ . . . .
- ☐ . . . .

TUESDAY
KITCHEN DAY

- ☐ . . . .
- ☐ . . . .
- ☐ . . . .
- ☐ . . . .
- ☐ . . . .
- ☐ . . . .

WEDNESDAY
BEDROOM DAY

- ☐ . . . .
- ☐ . . . .
- ☐ . . . .
- ☐ . . . .
- ☐ . . . .
- ☐ . . . .

THUREDAY
LAUNDRY DAY

- ☐ . . . .
- ☐ . . . .
- ☐ . . . .
- ☐ . . . .
- ☐ . . . .
- ☐ . . . .

FRIDAY
BATHROOM DAY

- ☐ . . . .
- ☐ . . . .
- ☐ . . . .
- ☐ . . . .
- ☐ . . . .
- ☐ . . . .

SATURDAY
OUTSIDE

- ☐ . . . .
- ☐ . . . .
- ☐ . . . .
- ☐ . . . .
- ☐ . . . .
- ☐ . . . .

TO DO LIST EVERY DAY

- [ ] . . . .
- [ ] . . . .
- [ ] . . . .
- [ ] . . . .
- [ ] . . . .
- [ ] . . . .
- [ ] . . . .
- [ ] . . . .
- [ ] . . . .
- [ ] . . . .
- [ ] . . . .
- [ ] . . . .
- [ ] . . . .
- [ ] . . . .
- [ ] . . . .

NOTES

 # CLEANING TRACK

MONDAY
LIVING ROOM DAY

TUESDAY
KITCHEN DAY

WEDNESDAY
BEDROOM DAY

THUREDAY
LAUNDRY DAY

FRIDAY
BATHROOM DAY

SATURDAY
OUTSIDE

TO DO LIST EVERY DAY

- [ ] . . . .
- [ ] . . . .
- [ ] . . . .
- [ ] . . . .
- [ ] . . . .
- [ ] . . . .
- [ ] . . . .
- [ ] . . . .
- [ ] . . . .
- [ ] . . . .
- [ ] . . . .
- [ ] . . . .
- [ ] . . . .

NOTES

 # CLEANING TRACK

MONDAY
LIVING ROOM DAY

- □ . . . .
- □ . . . .
- □ . . . .
- □ . . . .
- □ . . . .
- □ . . . .

TUESDAY
KITCHEN DAY

- □ . . . .
- □ . . . .
- □ . . . .
- □ . . . .
- □ . . . .
- □ . . . .

WEDNESDAY
BEDROOM DAY

- □ . . . .
- □ . . . .
- □ . . . .
- □ . . . .
- □ . . . .

THUREDAY
LAUNDRY DAY

- □ . . . .
- □ . . . .
- □ . . . .
- □ . . . .
- □ . . . .

FRIDAY
BATHROOM DAY

- □ . . . .
- □ . . . .
- □ . . . .
- □ . . . .
- □ . . . .

SATURDAY
OUTSIDE

- □ . . . .
- □ . . . .
- □ . . . .
- □ . . . .
- □ . . . .
- □ . . . .

TO DO LIST EVERY DAY

- ☐ . . . .
- ☐ . . . .
- ☐ . . . .
- ☐ . . . .
- ☐ . . . .
- ☐ . . . .
- ☐ . . . .
- ☐ . . . .
- ☐ . . . .
- ☐ . . . .
- ☐ . . . .
- ☐ . . . .
- ☐ . . . .
- ☐ . . . .
- ☐ . . . .

NOTES

 # CLEANING TRACK

MONDAY
LIVING ROOM DAY

- ....
- ....
- ....
- ....
- ....
- ....

TUESDAY
KITCHEN DAY

- ....
- ....
- ....
- ....
- ....
- ....

WEDNESDAY
BEDROOM DAY

- ....
- ....
- ....
- ....
- ....
- ....

THUREDAY
LAUNDRY DAY

- ....
- ....
- ....
- ....
- ....
- ....

FRIDAY
BATHROOM DAY

- ....
- ....
- ....
- ....
- ....
- ....

SATURDAY
OUTSIDE

- ....
- ....
- ....
- ....
- ....
- ....

TO DO LIST EVERY DAY

- ☐ . . . .
- ☐ . . . .
- ☐ . . . .
- ☐ . . . .
- ☐ . . . .
- ☐ . . . .
- ☐ . . . .
- ☐ . . . .
- ☐ . . . .
- ☐ . . . .
- ☐ . . . .
- ☐ . . . .
- ☐ . . . .
- ☐ . . . .
- ☐ . . . .

NOTES

 # CLEANING TRACK

MONDAY
LIVING ROOM DAY

- ☐ . . . .
- ☐ . . . .
- ☐ . . . .
- ☐ . . . .
- ☐ . . . .
- ☐ . . . .

TUESDAY
KITCHEN DAY

- ☐ . . . .
- ☐ . . . .
- ☐ . . . .
- ☐ . . . .
- ☐ . . . .
- ☐ . . . .

WEDNESDAY
BEDROOM DAY

- ☐ . . . .
- ☐ . . . .
- ☐ . . . .
- ☐ . . . .
- ☐ . . . .
- ☐ . . . .

THUREDAY
LAUNDRY DAY

- ☐ . . . .
- ☐ . . . .
- ☐ . . . .
- ☐ . . . .
- ☐ . . . .
- ☐ . . . .

FRIDAY
BATHROOM DAY

- ☐ . . . .
- ☐ . . . .
- ☐ . . . .
- ☐ . . . .
- ☐ . . . .
- ☐ . . . .

SATURDAY
OUTSIDE

- ☐ . . . .
- ☐ . . . .
- ☐ . . . .
- ☐ . . . .
- ☐ . . . .

TO DO LIST EVERY DAY

- ....
- ....
- ....
- ....
- ....
- ....
- ....
- ....
- ....
- ....
- ....
- ....
- ....
- ....

NOTES

 # CLEANING TRACK

MONDAY
LIVING ROOM DAY

☐ . . . .
☐ . . . .
☐ . . . .
☐ . . . .
☐ . . . .
☐ . . . .

TUESDAY
KITCHEN DAY

☐ . . . .
☐ . . . .
☐ . . . .
☐ . . . .
☐ . . . .
☐ . . . .

WEDNESDAY
BEDROOM DAY

☐ . . . .
☐ . . . .
☐ . . . .
☐ . . . .
☐ . . . .
☐ . . . .

THUREDAY
LAUNDRY DAY

☐ . . . .
☐ . . . .
☐ . . . .
☐ . . . .
☐ . . . .
☐ . . . .

FRIDAY
BATHROOM DAY

☐ . . . .
☐ . . . .
☐ . . . .
☐ . . . .
☐ . . . .
☐ . . . .

SATURDAY
OUTSIDE

☐ . . . .
☐ . . . .
☐ . . . .
☐ . . . .
☐ . . . .
☐ . . . .

TO DO LIST EVERY DAY

- ⬜ . . . .
- ⬜ . . . .
- ⬜ . . . .
- ⬜ . . . .
- ⬜ . . . .
- ⬜ . . . .
- ⬜ . . . .
- ⬜ . . . .
- ⬜ . . . .
- ⬜ . . . .
- ⬜ . . . .
- ⬜ . . . .
- ⬜ . . . .
- ⬜ . . . .
- ⬜ . . . .

NOTES

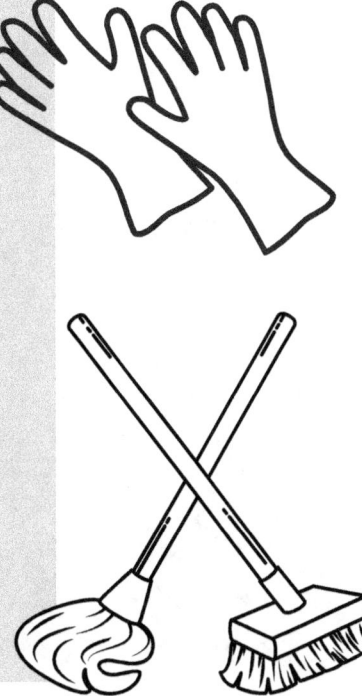

 # CLEANING TRACK

MONDAY
LIVING ROOM DAY

- ....
- ....
- ....
- ....
- ....
- ....

TUESDAY
KITCHEN DAY

- ....
- ....
- ....
- ....
- ....
- ....

WEDNESDAY
BEDROOM DAY

- ....
- ....
- ....
- ....
- ....
- ....

THUREDAY
LAUNDRY DAY

- ....
- ....
- ....
- ....
- ....
- ....

FRIDAY
BATHROOM DAY

- ....
- ....
- ....
- ....
- ....
- ....

SATURDAY
OUTSIDE

- ....
- ....
- ....
- ....
- ....
- ....

TO DO LIST EVERY DAY

- ....
- ....
- ....
- ....
- ....
- ....
- ....
- ....
- ....
- ....
- ....
- ....
- ....
- ....
- ....
- ....

NOTES

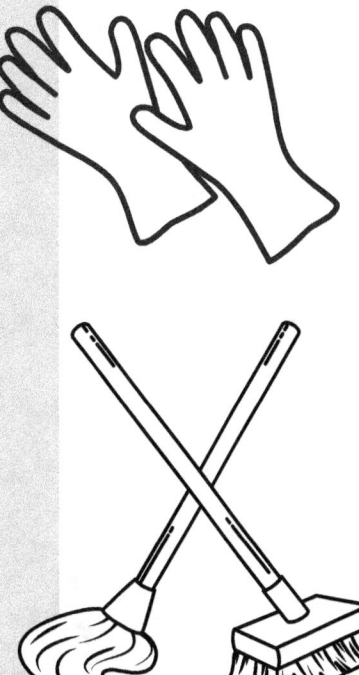

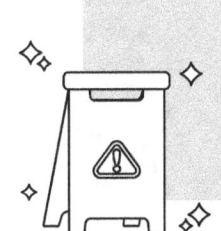

 # CLEANING TRACK

MONDAY
LIVING ROOM DAY

- ·
- ·
- ·
- ·
- ·
- ·

TUESDAY
KITCHEN DAY

- ·
- ·
- ·
- ·
- ·
- ·

WEDNESDAY
BEDROOM DAY

- ·
- ·
- ·
- ·
- ·
- ·

THUREDAY
LAUNDRY DAY

- ·
- ·
- ·
- ·
- ·
- ·

FRIDAY
BATHROOM DAY

- ·
- ·
- ·
- ·
- ·
- ·

SATURDAY
OUTSIDE

TO DO LIST EVERY DAY

- [ ] . . . .
- [ ] . . . .
- [ ] . . . .
- [ ] . . . .
- [ ] . . . .
- [ ] . . . .
- [ ] . . . .
- [ ] . . . .
- [ ] . . . .
- [ ] . . . .
- [ ] . . . .
- [ ] . . . .
- [ ] . . . .
- [ ] . . . .
- [ ] . . . .

NOTES

 # CLEANING TRACK

MONDAY
LIVING ROOM DAY

- . . . .
- . . . .
- . . . .
- . . . .
- . . . .
- . . . .

TUESDAY
KITCHEN DAY

- . . . .
- . . . .
- . . . .
- . . . .
- . . . .
- . . . .

WEDNESDAY
BEDROOM DAY

- . . . .
- . . . .
- . . . .
- . . . .
- . . . .
- . . . .

THUREDAY
LAUNDRY DAY

- . . . .
- . . . .
- . . . .
- . . . .
- . . . .
- . . . .

FRIDAY
BATHROOM DAY

- . . . .
- . . . .
- . . . .
- . . . .
- . . . .

SATURDAY
OUTSIDE

- . . . .
- . . . .
- . . . .
- . . . .
- . . . .

TO DO LIST EVERY DAY

- □ . . . .
- □ . . . .
- □ . . . .
- □ . . . .
- □ . . . .
- □ . . . .
- □ . . . .
- □ . . . .
- □ . . . .
- □ . . . .
- □ . . . .
- □ . . . .
- □ . . . .
- □ . . . .
- □ . . . .

NOTES

CLEANING TRACK

MONDAY
LIVING ROOM DAY

- . . . .
- . . . .
- . . . .
- . . . .
- . . . .
- . . . .

TUESDAY
KITCHEN DAY

- . . . .
- . . . .
- . . . .
- . . . .
- . . . .
- . . . .

WEDNESDAY
BEDROOM DAY

- . . . .
- . . . .
- . . . .
- . . . .
- . . . .
- . . . .

THUREDAY
LAUNDRY DAY

- . . . .
- . . . .
- . . . .
- . . . .
- . . . .
- . . . .

FRIDAY
BATHROOM DAY

- . . . .
- . . . .
- . . . .
- . . . .
- . . . .

SATURDAY
OUTSIDE

- . . . .
- . . . .
- . . . .
- . . . .
- . . . .

TO DO LIST EVERY DAY

- ☐ ....
- ☐ ....
- ☐ ....
- ☐ ....
- ☐ ....
- ☐ ....
- ☐ ....
- ☐ ....
- ☐ ....
- ☐ ....
- ☐ ....
- ☐ ....
- ☐ ....
- ☐ ....
- ☐ ....
- ☐ ....

NOTES

CLEANING TRACK

MONDAY
LIVING ROOM DAY

- ☐ ....
- ☐ ....
- ☐ ....
- ☐ ....
- ☐ ....
- ☐ ....

TUESDAY
KITCHEN DAY

- ☐ ....
- ☐ ....
- ☐ ....
- ☐ ....
- ☐ ....
- ☐ ....

WEDNESDAY
BEDROOM DAY

- ☐ ....
- ☐ ....
- ☐ ....
- ☐ ....
- ☐ ....
- ☐ ....

THUREDAY
LAUNDRY DAY

- ☐ ....
- ☐ ....
- ☐ ....
- ☐ ....
- ☐ ....
- ☐ ....

FRIDAY
BATHROOM DAY

- ☐ ....
- ☐ ....
- ☐ ....
- ☐ ....
- ☐ ....

SATURDAY
OUTSIDE

- ☐ ....
- ☐ ....
- ☐ ....
- ☐ ....
- ☐ ....

TO DO LIST EVERY DAY

- ☐ . . . .
- ☐ . . . .
- ☐ . . . .
- ☐ . . . .
- ☐ . . . .
- ☐ . . . .
- ☐ . . . .
- ☐ . . . .
- ☐ . . . .
- ☐ . . . .
- ☐ . . . .
- ☐ . . . .
- ☐ . . . .
- ☐ . . . .
- ☐ . . . .

NOTES

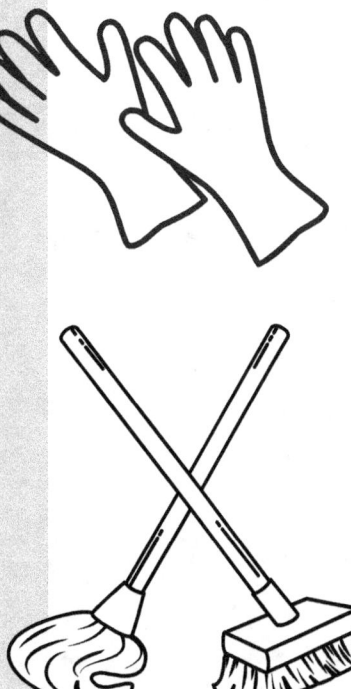

 # CLEANING TRACK

MONDAY
LIVING ROOM DAY

- ....
- ....
- ....
- ....
- ....
- ....

TUESDAY
KITCHEN DAY

- ....
- ....
- ....
- ....
- ....
- ....

WEDNESDAY
BEDROOM DAY

- ....
- ....
- ....
- ....
- ....

THUREDAY
LAUNDRY DAY

- ....
- ....
- ....
- ....
- ....

FRIDAY
BATHROOM DAY

- ....
- ....
- ....
- ....
- ....

SATURDAY
OUTSIDE

- ....
- ....
- ....
- ....
- ....

TO DO LIST EVERY DAY

- [ ] ....
- [ ] ....
- [ ] ....
- [ ] ....
- [ ] ....
- [ ] ....
- [ ] ....
- [ ] ....
- [ ] ....
- [ ] ....
- [ ] ....
- [ ] ....
- [ ] ....
- [ ] ....
- [ ] ....

NOTES

CLEANING TRACK

MONDAY
LIVING ROOM DAY

- ☐ . . . .
- ☐ . . . .
- ☐ . . . .
- ☐ . . . .
- ☐ . . . .
- ☐ . . . .

TUESDAY
KITCHEN DAY

- ☐ . . . .
- ☐ . . . .
- ☐ . . . .
- ☐ . . . .
- ☐ . . . .
- ☐ . . . .

WEDNESDAY
BEDROOM DAY

- ☐ . . . .
- ☐ . . . .
- ☐ . . . .
- ☐ . . . .
- ☐ . . . .
- ☐ . . . .

THUREDAY
LAUNDRY DAY

- ☐ . . . .
- ☐ . . . .
- ☐ . . . .
- ☐ . . . .
- ☐ . . . .
- ☐ . . . .

FRIDAY
BATHROOM DAY

- ☐ . . . .
- ☐ . . . .
- ☐ . . . .
- ☐ . . . .
- ☐ . . . .
- ☐ . . . .

SATURDAY
OUTSIDE

- ☐ . . . .
- ☐ . . . .
- ☐ . . . .
- ☐ . . . .
- ☐ . . . .
- ☐ . . . .

TO DO LIST EVERY DAY

- ☐ . . . .
- ☐ . . . .
- ☐ . . . .
- ☐ . . . .
- ☐ . . . .
- ☐ . . . .
- ☐ . . . .
- ☐ . . . .
- ☐ . . . .
- ☐ . . . .
- ☐ . . . .
- ☐ . . . .
- ☐ . . . .
- ☐ . . . .
- ☐ . . . .

NOTES

 # CLEANING TRACK

MONDAY
LIVING ROOM DAY

- ▪ . . . .
- ▪ . . . .
- ▪ . . . .
- ▪ . . . .
- ▪ . . . .
- ▪ . . . .

TUESDAY
KITCHEN DAY

- ▪ . . . .
- ▪ . . . .
- ▪ . . . .
- ▪ . . . .
- ▪ . . . .
- ▪ . . . .

WEDNESDAY
BEDROOM DAY

- ▪ . . . .
- ▪ . . . .
- ▪ . . . .
- ▪ . . . .
- ▪ . . . .
- ▪ . . . .

THUREDAY
LAUNDRY DAY

- ▪ . . . .
- ▪ . . . .
- ▪ . . . .
- ▪ . . . .
- ▪ . . . .
- ▪ . . . .

FRIDAY
BATHROOM DAY

- ▪ . . . .
- ▪ . . . .
- ▪ . . . .
- ▪ . . . .
- ▪ . . . .
- ▪ . . . .

SATURDAY
OUTSIDE

- ▪ . . . .
- ▪ . . . .
- ▪ . . . .
- ▪ . . . .
- ▪ . . . .
- ▪ . . . .

TO DO LIST EVERY DAY

- [ ] . . . .
- [ ] . . . .
- [ ] . . . .
- [ ] . . . .
- [ ] . . . .
- [ ] . . . .
- [ ] . . . .
- [ ] . . . .
- [ ] . . . .
- [ ] . . . .
- [ ] . . . .
- [ ] . . . .
- [ ] . . . .
- [ ] . . . .
- [ ] . . . .
- [ ] . . . .

NOTES

 # CLEANING TRACK

MONDAY
LIVING ROOM DAY

· ·
· ·
· ·
· ·
· ·
· ·

TUESDAY
KITCHEN DAY

· ·
· ·
· ·
· ·
· ·
· ·

WEDNESDAY
BEDROOM DAY

· ·
· ·
· ·
· ·
· ·
· ·

THUREDAY
LAUNDRY DAY

· ·
· ·
· ·
· ·
· ·
· ·

FRIDAY
BATHROOM DAY

· ·
· ·
· ·
· ·
· ·
· ·

SATURDAY
OUTSIDE

· ·
· ·
· ·
· ·
· ·
· ·

TO DO LIST EVERY DAY

- □ . . . .
- □ . . . .
- □ . . . .
- □ . . . .
- □ . . . .
- □ . . . .
- □ . . . .
- □ . . . .
- □ . . . .
- □ . . . .
- □ . . . .
- □ . . . .
- □ . . . .
- □ . . . .
- □ . . . .
- □ . . . .

NOTES

 # CLEANING TRACK

MONDAY
LIVING ROOM DAY

- . . . .
- . . . .
- . . . .
- . . . .
- . . . .
- . . . .
- . . . .

TUESDAY
KITCHEN DAY

- . . . .
- . . . .
- . . . .
- . . . .
- . . . .
- . . . .
- . . . .

WEDNESDAY
BEDROOM DAY

- . . . .
- . . . .
- . . . .
- . . . .
- . . . .
- . . . .

THUREDAY
LAUNDRY DAY

- . . . .
- . . . .
- . . . .
- . . . .
- . . . .
- . . . .

FRIDAY
BATHROOM DAY

- . . . .
- . . . .
- . . . .
- . . . .
- . . . .
- . . . .

SATURDAY
OUTSIDE

- . . . .
- . . . .
- . . . .
- . . . .
- . . . .
- . . . .

TO DO LIST EVERY DAY

- ·
- ·
- ·
- ·
- ·
- ·
- ·
- ·
- ·
- ·
- ·
- ·
- ·
- ·

NOTES

CLEANING TRACK

MONDAY
LIVING ROOM DAY

- ·
- ·
- ·
- ·
- ·
- ·

TUESDAY
KITCHEN DAY

- ·
- ·
- ·
- ·
- ·
- ·

WEDNESDAY
BEDROOM DAY

- ·
- ·
- ·
- ·
- ·
- ·

THUREDAY
LAUNDRY DAY

- ·
- ·
- ·
- ·
- ·
- ·

FRIDAY
BATHROOM DAY

- ·
- ·
- ·
- ·
- ·

SATURDAY
OUTSIDE

- ·
- ·
- ·
- ·
- ·

TO DO LIST EVERY DAY

NOTES

 # CLEANING TRACK

MONDAY
LIVING ROOM DAY

- . . . .
- . . . .
- . . . .
- . . . .
- . . . .
- . . . .

TUESDAY
KITCHEN DAY

- . . . .
- . . . .
- . . . .
- . . . .
- . . . .
- . . . .

WEDNESDAY
BEDROOM DAY

- . . . .
- . . . .
- . . . .
- . . . .
- . . . .
- . . . .

THUREDAY
LAUNDRY DAY

- . . . .
- . . . .
- . . . .
- . . . .
- . . . .
- . . . .

FRIDAY
BATHROOM DAY

- . . . .
- . . . .
- . . . .
- . . . .
- . . . .

SATURDAY
OUTSIDE

- . . . .
- . . . .
- . . . .
- . . . .
- . . . .

TO DO LIST EVERY DAY

- ☐ ·
- ☐ ·
- ☐ ·
- ☐ ·
- ☐ ·
- ☐ ·
- ☐ ·
- ☐ ·
- ☐ ·
- ☐ ·
- ☐ ·
- ☐ ·
- ☐ ·
- ☐ ·
- ☐ ·

NOTES

 # CLEANING TRACK

MONDAY
LIVING ROOM DAY

- [ ] ....
- [ ] ....
- [ ] ....
- [ ] ....
- [ ] ....
- [ ] ....

TUESDAY
KITCHEN DAY

- [ ] ....
- [ ] ....
- [ ] ....
- [ ] ....
- [ ] ....
- [ ] ....

WEDNESDAY
BEDROOM DAY

- [ ] ....
- [ ] ....
- [ ] ....
- [ ] ....
- [ ] ....

THUREDAY
LAUNDRY DAY

- [ ] ....
- [ ] ....
- [ ] ....
- [ ] ....
- [ ] ....

FRIDAY
BATHROOM DAY

- [ ] ....
- [ ] ....
- [ ] ....
- [ ] ....
- [ ] ....

SATURDAY
OUTSIDE

- [ ] ....
- [ ] ....
- [ ] ....
- [ ] ....
- [ ] ....

TO DO LIST EVERY DAY

- ....
- ....
- ....
- ....
- ....
- ....
- ....
- ....
- ....
- ....
- ....
- ....
- ....
- ....
- ....

NOTES

 # CLEANING TRACK

MONDAY
LIVING ROOM DAY

- ....
- ....
- ....
- ....
- ....
- ....

TUESDAY
KITCHEN DAY

- ....
- ....
- ....
- ....
- ....
- ....

WEDNESDAY
BEDROOM DAY

- ....
- ....
- ....
- ....
- ....
- ....

THUREDAY
LAUNDRY DAY

- ....
- ....
- ....
- ....
- ....
- ....

FRIDAY
BATHROOM DAY

- ....
- ....
- ....
- ....
- ....

SATURDAY
OUTSIDE

- ....
- ....
- ....
- ....
- ....

TO DO LIST EVERY DAY

- ☐ . . . .
- ☐ . . . .
- ☐ . . . .
- ☐ . . . .
- ☐ . . . .
- ☐ . . . .
- ☐ . . . .
- ☐ . . . .
- ☐ . . . .
- ☐ . . . .
- ☐ . . . .
- ☐ . . . .
- ☐ . . . .
- ☐ . . . .
- ☐ . . . .

NOTES

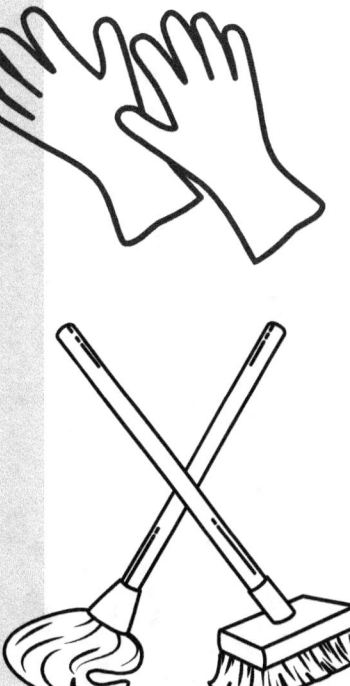

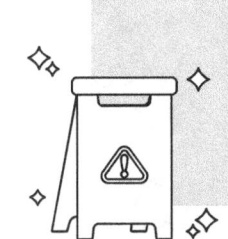

 # CLEANING TRACK

MONDAY
LIVING ROOM DAY

- [ ] . . . .
- [ ] . . . .
- [ ] . . . .
- [ ] . . . .
- [ ] . . . .
- [ ] . . . .

TUESDAY
KITCHEN DAY

- [ ] . . . .
- [ ] . . . .
- [ ] . . . .
- [ ] . . . .
- [ ] . . . .
- [ ] . . . .

WEDNESDAY
BEDROOM DAY

- [ ] . . . .
- [ ] . . . .
- [ ] . . . .
- [ ] . . . .
- [ ] . . . .
- [ ] . . . .

THUREDAY
LAUNDRY DAY

- [ ] . . . .
- [ ] . . . .
- [ ] . . . .
- [ ] . . . .
- [ ] . . . .
- [ ] . . . .

FRIDAY
BATHROOM DAY

- [ ] . . . .
- [ ] . . . .
- [ ] . . . .
- [ ] . . . .
- [ ] . . . .
- [ ] . . . .

SATURDAY
OUTSIDE

- [ ] . . . .
- [ ] . . . .
- [ ] . . . .
- [ ] . . . .
- [ ] . . . .
- [ ] . . . .

TO DO LIST EVERY DAY

- ☐ ....
- ☐ ....
- ☐ ....
- ☐ ....
- ☐ ....
- ☐ ....
- ☐ ....
- ☐ ....
- ☐ ....
- ☐ ....
- ☐ ....
- ☐ ....
- ☐ ....
- ☐ ....
- ☐ ....
- ☐ ....

NOTES

CLEANING TRACK

MONDAY
LIVING ROOM DAY

- [ ] . . . .
- [ ] . . . .
- [ ] . . . .
- [ ] . . . .
- [ ] . . . .
- [ ] . . . .

TUESDAY
KITCHEN DAY

- [ ] . . . .
- [ ] . . . .
- [ ] . . . .
- [ ] . . . .
- [ ] . . . .
- [ ] . . . .

WEDNESDAY
BEDROOM DAY

- [ ] . . . .
- [ ] . . . .
- [ ] . . . .
- [ ] . . . .
- [ ] . . . .
- [ ] . . . .

THUREDAY
LAUNDRY DAY

- [ ] . . . .
- [ ] . . . .
- [ ] . . . .
- [ ] . . . .
- [ ] . . . .

FRIDAY
BATHROOM DAY

- [ ] . . . .
- [ ] . . . .
- [ ] . . . .
- [ ] . . . .
- [ ] . . . .

SATURDAY
OUTSIDE

- [ ] . . . .
- [ ] . . . .
- [ ] . . . .
- [ ] . . . .

TO DO LIST EVERY DAY

- ·
- ·
- ·
- ·
- ·
- ·
- ·
- ·
- ·
- ·
- ·
- ·
- ·
- ·
- ·

NOTES

CLEANING TRACK

MONDAY
LIVING ROOM DAY

- ....
- ....
- ....
- ....
- ....
- ....

TUESDAY
KITCHEN DAY

- ....
- ....
- ....
- ....
- ....
- ....

WEDNESDAY
BEDROOM DAY

- ....
- ....
- ....
- ....
- ....
- ....

THUREDAY
LAUNDRY DAY

- ....
- ....
- ....
- ....
- ....
- ....

FRIDAY
BATHROOM DAY

- ....
- ....
- ....
- ....
- ....

SATURDAY
OUTSIDE

- ....
- ....
- ....
- ....
- ....

TO DO LIST EVERY DAY

- ☐ . . . .
- ☐ . . . .
- ☐ . . . .
- ☐ . . . .
- ☐ . . . .
- ☐ . . . .
- ☐ . . . .
- ☐ . . . .
- ☐ . . . .
- ☐ . . . .
- ☐ . . . .
- ☐ . . . .
- ☐ . . . .
- ☐ . . . .
- ☐ . . . .

NOTES

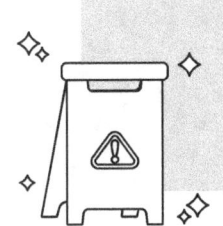

 # CLEANING TRACK

MONDAY
LIVING ROOM DAY

- [ ] ·
- [ ] ·
- [ ] ·
- [ ] ·
- [ ] ·
- [ ] ·

TUESDAY
KITCHEN DAY

- [ ] ·
- [ ] ·
- [ ] ·
- [ ] ·
- [ ] ·
- [ ] ·

WEDNESDAY
BEDROOM DAY

- [ ] ·
- [ ] ·
- [ ] ·
- [ ] ·
- [ ] ·
- [ ] ·

THUREDAY
LAUNDRY DAY

- [ ] ·
- [ ] ·
- [ ] ·
- [ ] ·
- [ ] ·
- [ ] ·

FRIDAY
BATHROOM DAY

- [ ] ·
- [ ] ·
- [ ] ·
- [ ] ·
- [ ] ·

SATURDAY
OUTSIDE

- [ ] ·
- [ ] ·
- [ ] ·
- [ ] ·
- [ ] ·

TO DO LIST EVERY DAY

- [ ] . . . .
- [ ] . . . .
- [ ] . . . .
- [ ] . . . .
- [ ] . . . .
- [ ] . . . .
- [ ] . . . .
- [ ] . . . .
- [ ] . . . .
- [ ] . . . .
- [ ] . . . .
- [ ] . . . .
- [ ] . . . .
- [ ] . . . .
- [ ] . . . .

NOTES

CLEANING TRACK

MONDAY
LIVING ROOM DAY

TUESDAY
KITCHEN DAY

WEDNESDAY
BEDROOM DAY

THUREDAY
LAUNDRY DAY

FRIDAY
BATHROOM DAY

SATURDAY
OUTSIDE

TO DO LIST EVERY DAY

- [ ] . . . .
- [ ] . . . .
- [ ] . . . .
- [ ] . . . .
- [ ] . . . .
- [ ] . . . .
- [ ] . . . .
- [ ] . . . .
- [ ] . . . .
- [ ] . . . .
- [ ] . . . .
- [ ] . . . .
- [ ] . . . .
- [ ] . . . .

NOTES

 # CLEANING TRACK

MONDAY
LIVING ROOM DAY

- ·
- ·
- ·
- ·
- ·
- ·

TUESDAY
KITCHEN DAY

- ·
- ·
- ·
- ·
- ·
- ·

WEDNESDAY
BEDROOM DAY

- ·
- ·
- ·
- ·
- ·
- ·

THUREDAY
LAUNDRY DAY

- ·
- ·
- ·
- ·
- ·
- ·

FRIDAY
BATHROOM DAY

- ·
- ·
- ·
- ·
- ·
- ·

SATURDAY
OUTSIDE

- ·
- ·
- ·
- ·
- ·
- ·

TO DO LIST EVERY DAY

- ....
- ....
- ....
- ....
- ....
- ....
- ....
- ....
- ....
- ....
- ....
- ....
- ....
- ....
- ....
- ....

NOTES

 # CLEANING TRACK

MONDAY
LIVING ROOM DAY

- ....
- ....
- ....
- ....
- ....
- ....

TUESDAY
KITCHEN DAY

- ....
- ....
- ....
- ....
- ....
- ....

WEDNESDAY
BEDROOM DAY

- ....
- ....
- ....
- ....
- ....
- ....

THUREDAY
LAUNDRY DAY

- ....
- ....
- ....
- ....
- ....
- ....

FRIDAY
BATHROOM DAY

- ....
- ....
- ....
- ....
- ....
- ....

SATURDAY
OUTSIDE

- ....
- ....
- ....
- ....
- ....
- ....

TO DO LIST EVERY DAY

NOTES

CLEANING TRACK

MONDAY
LIVING ROOM DAY

- [ ] . . . .
- [ ] . . . .
- [ ] . . . .
- [ ] . . . .
- [ ] . . . .
- [ ] . . . .

TUESDAY
KITCHEN DAY

- [ ] . . . .
- [ ] . . . .
- [ ] . . . .
- [ ] . . . .
- [ ] . . . .
- [ ] . . . .

WEDNESDAY
BEDROOM DAY

- [ ] . . . .
- [ ] . . . .
- [ ] . . . .
- [ ] . . . .
- [ ] . . . .
- [ ] . . . .

THUREDAY
LAUNDRY DAY

- [ ] . . . .
- [ ] . . . .
- [ ] . . . .
- [ ] . . . .
- [ ] . . . .
- [ ] . . . .

FRIDAY
BATHROOM DAY

- [ ] . . . .
- [ ] . . . .
- [ ] . . . .
- [ ] . . . .
- [ ] . . . .

SATURDAY
OUTSIDE

- [ ] . . . .
- [ ] . . . .
- [ ] . . . .
- [ ] . . . .
- [ ] . . . .

TO DO LIST EVERY DAY

- [ ] . . . .
- [ ] . . . .
- [ ] . . . .
- [ ] . . . .
- [ ] . . . .
- [ ] . . . .
- [ ] . . . .
- [ ] . . . .
- [ ] . . . .
- [ ] . . . .
- [ ] . . . .
- [ ] . . . .
- [ ] . . . .
- [ ] . . . .
- [ ] . . . .

NOTES

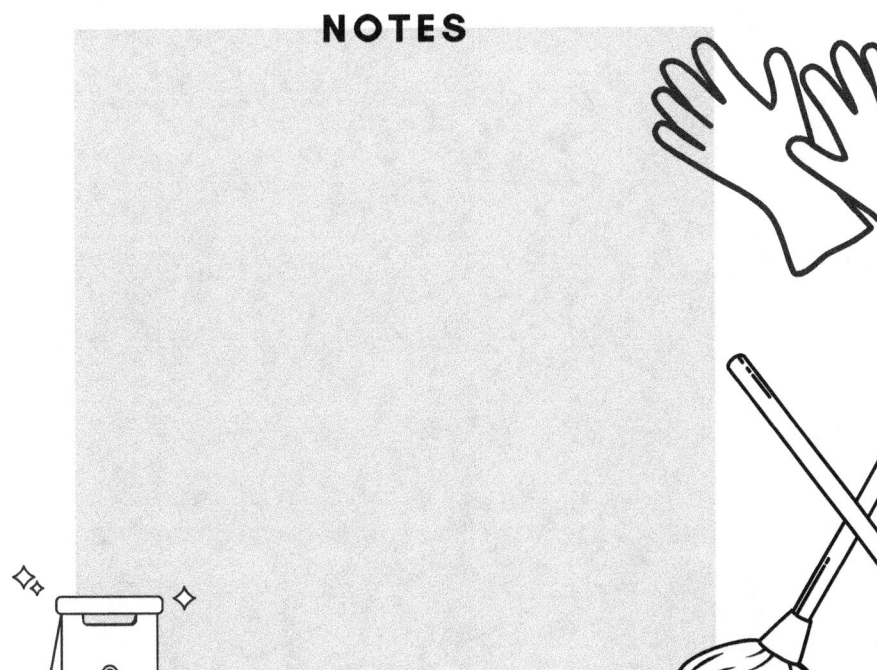
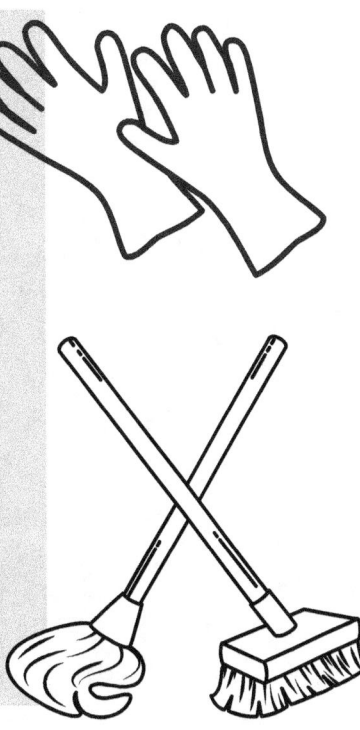

 # CLEANING TRACK

MONDAY
LIVING ROOM DAY

- ·
- ·
- ·
- ·
- ·
- ·

TUESDAY
KITCHEN DAY

- ·
- ·
- ·
- ·
- ·
- ·

WEDNESDAY
BEDROOM DAY

- ·
- ·
- ·
- ·
- ·
- ·

THUREDAY
LAUNDRY DAY

- ·
- ·
- ·
- ·
- ·
- ·

FRIDAY
BATHROOM DAY

- ·
- ·
- ·
- ·
- ·
- ·

SATURDAY
OUTSIDE

- ·
- ·
- ·
- ·
- ·
- ·

TO DO LIST EVERY DAY

- ....
- ....
- ....
- ....
- ....
- ....
- ....
- ....
- ....
- ....
- ....
- ....
- ....
- ....
- ....
- ....
- ....

NOTES

CLEANING TRACK

MONDAY
LIVING ROOM DAY

- [ ] . . . .
- [ ] . . . .
- [ ] . . . .
- [ ] . . . .
- [ ] . . . .
- [ ] . . . .

TUESDAY
KITCHEN DAY

- [ ] . . . .
- [ ] . . . .
- [ ] . . . .
- [ ] . . . .
- [ ] . . . .
- [ ] . . . .

WEDNESDAY
BEDROOM DAY

- [ ] . . . .
- [ ] . . . .
- [ ] . . . .
- [ ] . . . .
- [ ] . . . .
- [ ] . . . .

THUREDAY
LAUNDRY DAY

- [ ] . . . .
- [ ] . . . .
- [ ] . . . .
- [ ] . . . .
- [ ] . . . .
- [ ] . . . .

FRIDAY
BATHROOM DAY

- [ ] . . . .
- [ ] . . . .
- [ ] . . . .
- [ ] . . . .
- [ ] . . . .

SATURDAY
OUTSIDE

- [ ] . . . .
- [ ] . . . .
- [ ] . . . .
- [ ] . . . .
- [ ] . . . .

TO DO LIST EVERY DAY

- ☐ ·
- ☐ ·
- ☐ ·
- ☐ ·
- ☐ ·
- ☐ ·
- ☐ ·
- ☐ ·
- ☐ ·
- ☐ ·
- ☐ ·
- ☐ ·
- ☐ ·
- ☐ ·
- ☐ ·
- ☐ ·

NOTES

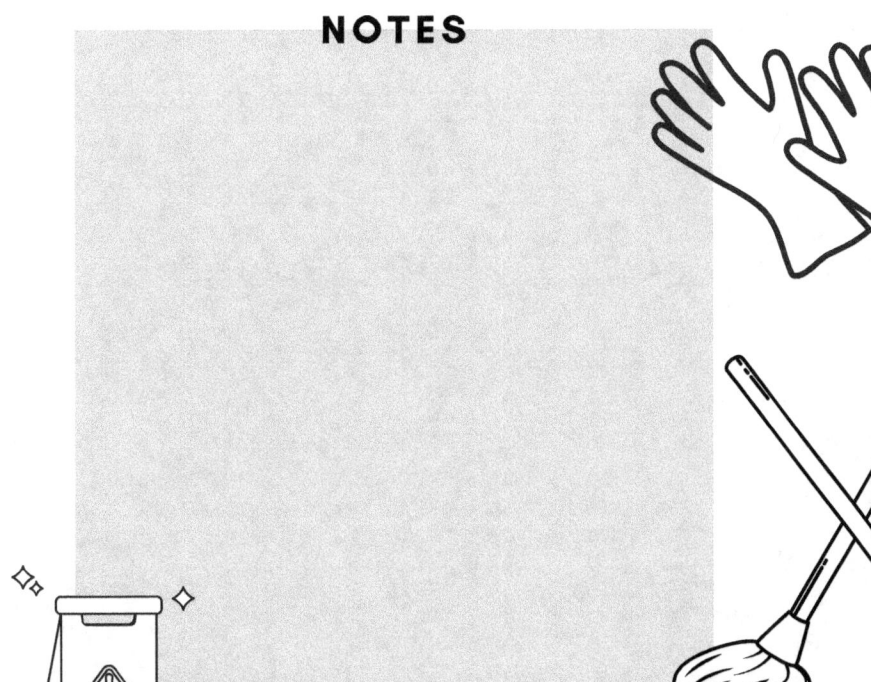
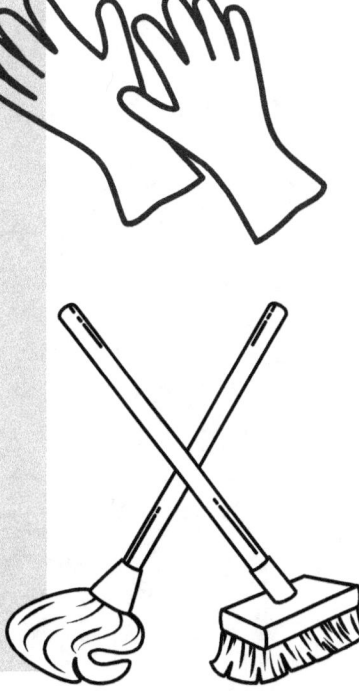

CLEANING TRACK

MONDAY
LIVING ROOM DAY

- ···
- ···
- ···
- ···
- ···
- ···

TUESDAY
KITCHEN DAY

- ···
- ···
- ···
- ···
- ···
- ···

WEDNESDAY
BEDROOM DAY

- ···
- ···
- ···
- ···
- ···

THUREDAY
LAUNDRY DAY

- ···
- ···
- ···
- ···
- ···

FRIDAY
BATHROOM DAY

- ···
- ···
- ···
- ···
- ···

SATURDAY
OUTSIDE

- ···
- ···
- ···
- ···
- ···

TO DO LIST EVERY DAY

- ....
- ....
- ....
- ....
- ....
- ....
- ....
- ....
- ....
- ....
- ....
- ....
- ....
- ....
- ....

NOTES

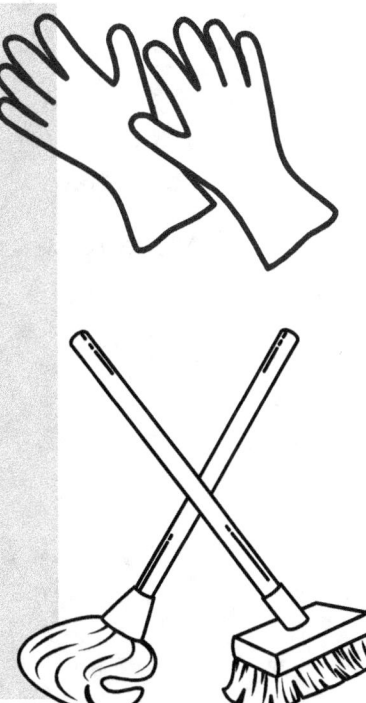

 # CLEANING TRACK

MONDAY
LIVING ROOM DAY

TUESDAY
KITCHEN DAY

WEDNESDAY
BEDROOM DAY

THUREDAY
LAUNDRY DAY

FRIDAY
BATHROOM DAY

SATURDAY
OUTSIDE

TO DO LIST EVERY DAY

- [ ] . . . .
- [ ] . . . .
- [ ] . . . .
- [ ] . . . .
- [ ] . . . .
- [ ] . . . .
- [ ] . . . .
- [ ] . . . .
- [ ] . . . .
- [ ] . . . .
- [ ] . . . .
- [ ] . . . .
- [ ] . . . .
- [ ] . . . .
- [ ] . . . .
- [ ] . . . .

NOTES

CLEANING TRACK

MONDAY
LIVING ROOM DAY

- [ ] ....
- [ ] ....
- [ ] ....
- [ ] ....
- [ ] ....
- [ ] ....

TUESDAY
KITCHEN DAY

- [ ] ....
- [ ] ....
- [ ] ....
- [ ] ....
- [ ] ....
- [ ] ....

WEDNESDAY
BEDROOM DAY

- [ ] ....
- [ ] ....
- [ ] ....
- [ ] ....
- [ ] ....
- [ ] ....

THUREDAY
LAUNDRY DAY

- [ ] ....
- [ ] ....
- [ ] ....
- [ ] ....
- [ ] ....
- [ ] ....

FRIDAY
BATHROOM DAY

- [ ] ....
- [ ] ....
- [ ] ....
- [ ] ....
- [ ] ....

SATURDAY
OUTSIDE

- [ ] ....
- [ ] ....
- [ ] ....
- [ ] ....
- [ ] ....

TO DO LIST EVERY DAY

- [ ] . . . .
- [ ] . . . .
- [ ] . . . .
- [ ] . . . .
- [ ] . . . .
- [ ] . . . .
- [ ] . . . .
- [ ] . . . .
- [ ] . . . .
- [ ] . . . .
- [ ] . . . .
- [ ] . . . .
- [ ] . . . .
- [ ] . . . .
- [ ] . . . .

NOTES

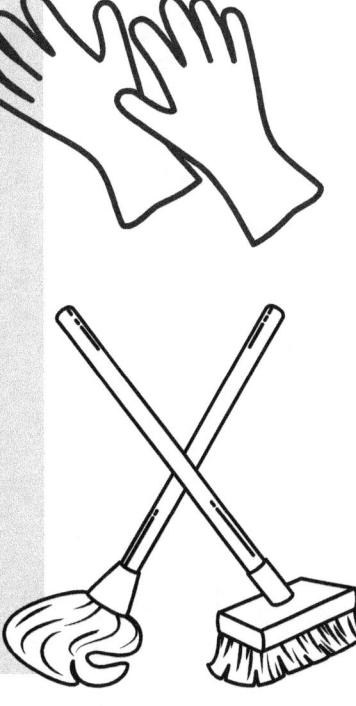

CLEANING TRACK

MONDAY
LIVING ROOM DAY

· ·
· ·
· ·
· ·
· ·
· ·

TUESDAY
KITCHEN DAY

· ·
· ·
· ·
· ·
· ·
· ·

WEDNESDAY
BEDROOM DAY

· ·
· ·
· ·
· ·
· ·
· ·

THUREDAY
LAUNDRY DAY

· ·
· ·
· ·
· ·
· ·
· ·

FRIDAY
BATHROOM DAY

· ·
· ·
· ·
· ·
· ·

SATURDAY
OUTSIDE

· ·
· ·
· ·
· ·
· ·

TO DO LIST EVERY DAY

- ☐ ·
- ☐ ·
- ☐ ·
- ☐ ·
- ☐ ·
- ☐ ·
- ☐ ·
- ☐ ·
- ☐ ·
- ☐ ·
- ☐ ·
- ☐ ·
- ☐ ·
- ☐ ·
- ☐ ·

NOTES

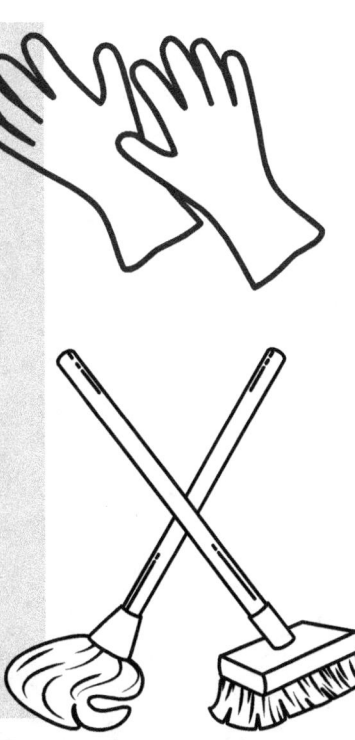

ULTIMATE HOUSEHOLD CHORES CHECKLIST

DAILY

TASK CHECKLIST

- SWEEPING AND MOPPING THE FLOOR
- VACUUMING THE RUGS AND CARPET
- WASHING DISHES AND KITCHENWARE
- CLEAN AND DISINFECT THE KITCHEN
- DOING LAUNDRY WASHING
- PREPARING AND COOKING MEALS

- FEEDING HOUSE PETS
- CLEANING PET LITTER
- CLEANING BATHROOMS
- DUSTING AND WIPING HOME FIXTURES
- TAKING OUT THE TRASH

WEEKLY

TASK CHECKLIST

- CHANGE AND WASH THE BEDDING
- DEEP CLEANING FLOORS AND CARPETS
- DEEP CLEANING THE BATHROOM
- DEEP CLEANING CLOTHES
- REPLACE RUGS, TOWELS AND CURTAINS
- WASHING THE CAR

MONTHLY

TASK CHECKLIST

- DEEP CLEANING WINDOWS
- DEEP CLEANING APPLIANCES
- BATHING AND GROOMING PETS
- VACUUMING FURNITURE AND CURTAINS
- CLEANING AND CHANGING WINDOW BLINDS

YEARLY

TASK CHECKLIST

- DEEP CLEANING THE CARPETS
- ORGANIZING THE STORAGE ROOM
- CLEAN AND ORGANIZE THE GARAGE
- DECLUTTER OLD ITEMS AND FIXTURES
- PRUNING TREES AND SHRUBS

Thank you!

We hope you enjoyed our book.

As a small family company, your feedback is very important to us .

Please let us know how you like our book at :

pickme.readme@gmail.com